I0814259

TALES FROM AMERICANA

Paul Bunyan and Babe the Blue Ox

BY HEATHER C. HUDAK

Kids Core
An Imprint of Abdo Publishing
abdobooks.com

abdobooks.com

Printed in the United States of America, North Mankato, Minnesota.
102023
012024

Cover Photo: Dave Rheaume Artist/iStockphoto
Interior Photos: iStockphoto, 4–5, 18, 28 (top); North Wind Picture Archives/Alamy, 6; Tom Clausen/Shutterstock Images, 8; Shutterstock Images, 10, 15, 29 (top); CSA-Printstock/DigitalVision Vectors/Getty Images, 12–13; David Brickner/Shutterstock Images, 16; Franck Fotos/Alamy, 20–21; Walt Disney Pictures/Everett Collection, 22, 28 (bottom); Red Line Editorial, 25; Ann Heisenfelt/AP Images, 26, 29 (bottom)

Editor: Angela Lim
Series Designer: Katharine Hale

Library of Congress Control Number: 2023939675

Publisher's Cataloging-in-Publication Data

Names: Hudak, Heather C., author.
Title: Paul Bunyan and Babe the Blue Ox / by Heather C. Hudak
Description: Minneapolis, Minnesota: Abdo Publishing, 2024 | Series: Tales from Americana | Includes online resources and index.
Identifiers: ISBN 9781098292867 (lib. bdg.) | ISBN 9798384910800 (ebook)
Subjects: LCSH: Bunyan, Paul (Legendary character)--Juvenile literature. | Logging--Juvenile literature. | Tall tales--Juvenile literature. | Folklore--Juvenile literature. | Lake States--Juvenile literature.
Classification: DDC 398.22--dc23

CONTENTS

Paul Bunyan was known for his giant size and strength.

CHAPTER 1

Tall Tales

Paul Bunyan was a powerful giant. He worked as a **lumberjack**. One winter, he and his crew set up to work next to a frozen river in Wisconsin. They cut down trees all winter. His **sidekick**, Babe the Blue Ox, hauled the trees to the river.

Oxen were often used to haul heavy logs.

The ice began melting in the spring. Paul Bunyan's crew prepared to tow the logs down the river. They would take the logs to the lumber mill to be processed. Before they left, Paul Bunyan washed his red long johns and hung them on a flagpole to dry. Then, he and his crew started their journey down the river.

After three days, they saw smoke rising in the distance. They realized it was a campfire from another logging camp. It looked a lot like their own camp. There were even red long johns hanging on a flagpole.

Paul Bunyan and his crew continued down the river. Three more days passed.

Logging Industry

In the 1600s, Europeans built settlements in what is now the United States and Canada. They cut down trees to clear land for farms and towns. They used the trees as lumber for buildings and ships. The timber trade became a leading industry.

Lumber mills process and cut logs. They produce lumber that can be used to make many products.

They came upon another logging camp. Another pair of red long johns hung on a flagpole. They laughed at how all the camps looked alike. But Paul Bunyan was upset.

There was not enough business in the area for all these lumberjacks. He stormed off to talk to the boss at the camp. When he got to the main building, he came across one of his own crew members.

Paul Bunyan realized he had been traveling along a round river. He and his crew had been going in circles! Paul Bunyan didn't want to be tricked by the river again. He grabbed a shovel. He went to the land in the middle of the river and dug a huge hole. He transformed the river into Round Lake.

American Folklore

Lumberjacks told stories about Paul Bunyan and Babe. These stories date back to the 1880s.

When stories of Paul Bunyan were first told in the 1880s, lumberjacks mostly used axes to cut down trees.

The first stories were told in northeastern Canada and the northeastern United States. These stories were passed down **orally** for many years.

"The Round River" was one of the first printed stories about Paul Bunyan. It ran in a Michigan newspaper in 1906. After that, other newspapers and book publishers began sharing stories about the giant lumberjack. People outside logging camps were introduced to Paul Bunyan and Babe the Blue Ox. Paul Bunyan was a **legend**.

Explore Online

Visit the website below. Does it give any new information about the job of a lumberjack that wasn't in Chapter One?

What Is a Log Jam?

abdocorelibrary.com/paul-bunyan-babe-blue-ox

Paul Bunyan spent most of his life outdoors.

CHAPTER 2

Mighty Lumberjack

Paul Bunyan is known for his giant size. When he was just one week old, Paul Bunyan was so big that he had to wear his father's clothes. When he was fully grown, Paul Bunyan was so big that he could live only outdoors. Paul Bunyan was very strong.

He could clear an entire forest with just one swing of his axe. He was also fast. At night, he could blow out his candle and jump into bed before the room became dark.

Meeting Babe

According to legend, Paul Bunyan met Babe on a cold winter night. He heard a sound coming from the snow. It had come from a baby ox.

Fact or Fiction?

Some historians think Paul Bunyan was based on a real person. One possible inspiration was a French Canadian man named Fabian Fournier. Fournier was born in the 1840s. He worked as a lumberjack in Michigan. He was about 6 feet (1.8 m) tall. This was much taller than average at the time.

Oxen typically grow to weigh about 1.5 tons (1.4 metric tons). Babe the Blue Ox was said to weigh 5 tons (4.5 metric tons).

The ox's fur had turned blue from the cold. Paul Bunyan took the ox home and warmed him by the fire. He named him Babe. After that, the two went everywhere together.

Legends say Paul Bunyan and Babe dug watering holes for lumberjacks to drink from. These became the Great Lakes.

Babe was tiny when Paul Bunyan found him. But he grew to be huge. Babe was also strong. He often helped Paul Bunyan by hauling lumber. Babe could even straighten winding roads.

Aside from their size, Paul Bunyan and Babe are known for the values they represent. They are hard workers. They stand up for their friends.

Paul Bunyan and Babe are said to have created many landmarks. For example, Paul Bunyan dragged his axe as he searched for firewood. This created the Grand Canyon. One time, Babe was towing a tank of water when it sprung a leak. The flowing water formed the Mississippi River.

Early Media

No one knows where stories about Paul Bunyan first started. Many places claim him as their own. These include Bemidji, Minnesota, and Bangor, Maine.

Paul Bunyan and Babe the Blue Ox were featured on a 1996 US stamp.

Around 1915, William Laughead created ads for a lumber company. The ads featured Paul Bunyan. Laughead came up with more stories. They were published in a 1922 book called *The Marvelous Exploits of Paul Bunyan*. These stories grew Paul Bunyan's popularity. Today, many people know about Paul Bunyan.

Primary Source

Michael Edmonds wrote a book about Paul Bunyan. He said early stories about Paul Bunyan often warned against the dangers of logging:

> The early stories are full of people who've lost a limb . . . and Bunyan is often coming to their rescue. He's their superhero.

Source: Jenny Peek. "Where and How the Tall Tales of Paul Bunyan and His Ax Began." *Wisconsin Public Radio*, 16 Dec. 2022, wpr.org. Accessed 16 May 2023.

Comparing Texts

Think about the quote. Does it support the information in this chapter? Or does it give a different perspective? Explain how in a few sentences.

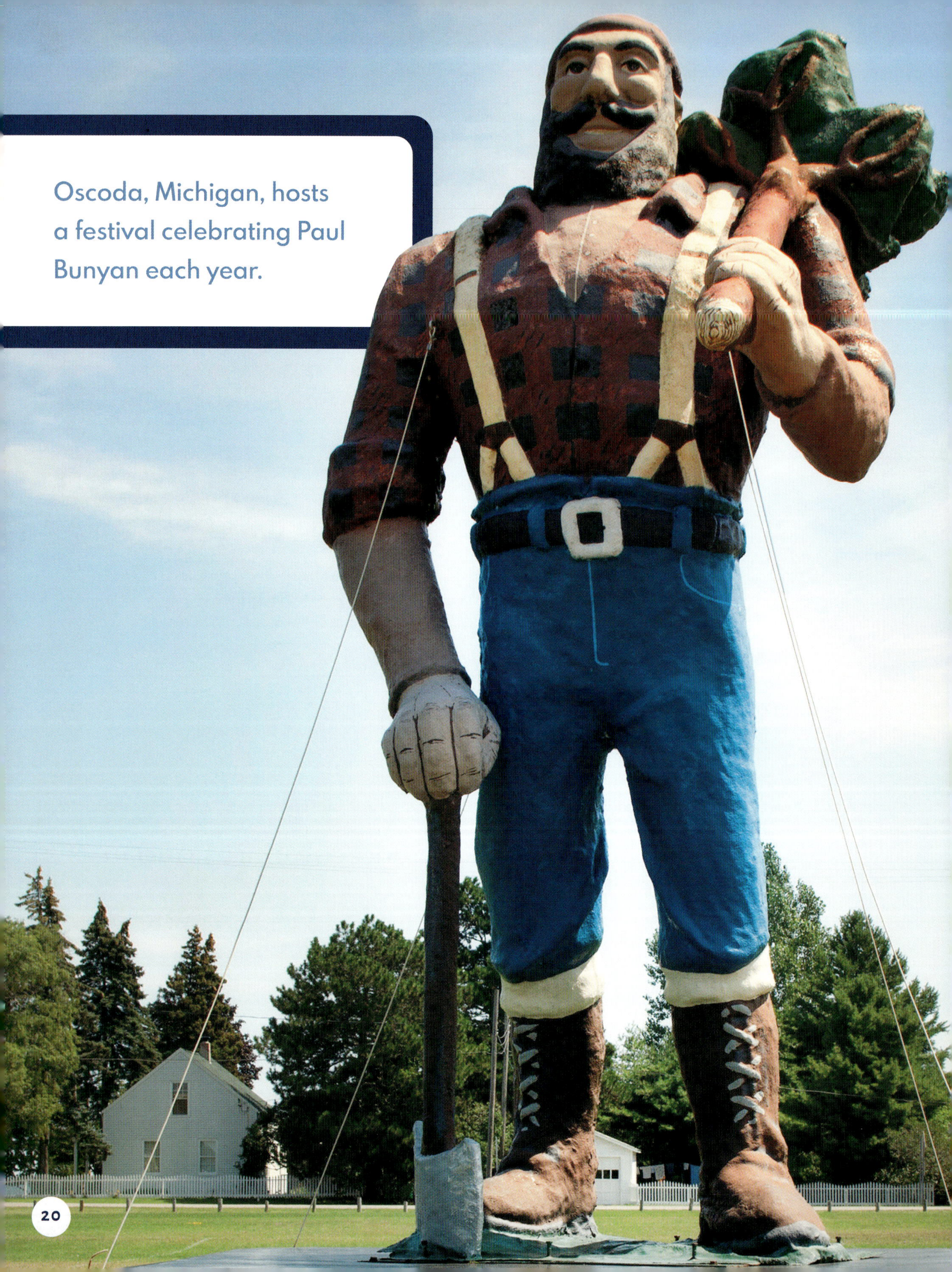

Oscoda, Michigan, hosts a festival celebrating Paul Bunyan each year.

CHAPTER 3

The Legend Lives On

Paul Bunyan is one of the best-known American folk heroes. Stories of Paul Bunyan are told around campfires and in classrooms today. Paul Bunyan has been featured in comics and cartoons.

Paul Bunyan was a friendly, hardworking lumberjack in Disney's short film about him.

Featured in Film

In 1958, Disney made a short, **animated** film about Paul Bunyan. In the film, a huge cradle washes ashore in Maine. There is a massive baby inside the cradle. The townspeople name the baby Paul Bunyan. They work together to care for him. This is different from other tales about Paul Bunyan. In many stories, five storks deliver Paul Bunyan to his parents.

The Disney film captures the strength Paul Bunyan is known for in the original legends. The townspeople give Paul Bunyan an axe for Christmas. He cuts down enough trees to last the town's sawmill a lifetime. The town grows quickly as a result.

Paul Bunyan also meets Babe the Blue Ox in the film. They work as a team to provide wood for many towns. But one day, the chainsaw is invented. It can cut trees faster than Paul Bunyan. Paul Bunyan and Babe are sad.

They move to Alaska and find joy in the outdoors. According to the film, the Northern Lights appear when Paul Bunyan and Babe are having fun.

Honoring a Legend

Statues of Paul Bunyan and Babe the Blue Ox are found across North America. A famous **monument** to these two legends is in Bemidji, Minnesota. The statues were built in 1937.

On with the Show

The Paul Bunyan Lumberjack Show performs at fairs and festivals all over the world. The show includes log rolling, chopping, sawing, and axe throwing.

Larger-Than-Life Statues

This map shows the locations of some of the statues built in honor of Paul Bunyan and Babe the Blue Ox.

These statues were added to the National Register of Historic Places in 1988.

National Paul Bunyan Day honors Paul Bunyan and Babe the Blue Ox. It is on June 28.

The Paul Bunyan statue in Bemidji, Minnesota, stands 18 feet (5.5 m) tall. The Babe statue is 10 feet (3 m) tall.

Many cities in North America celebrate the pair with festivals. Paul Bunyan Days Annual Festival takes place in Oscoda, Michigan. It has carnival rides, a wood carving competition, and food trucks. Each year, there is a parade and logging show for Paul Bunyan Days in Fort Bragg, California.

People have been telling tales of Paul Bunyan and Babe the Blue Ox for many years. The stories have changed over time. But many adventures of Paul Bunyan and Babe show the importance of hard work and friendship.

Further Evidence

Look at the website below. Does it give any new evidence to support Chapter Three?

Building the Legend

abdocorelibrary.com/paul-bunyan-babe-blue-ox

Legendary Facts

Paul Bunyan was known for his giant size.

Disney made a short animated film about Paul Bunyan in 1958.

Lumberjacks passed down stories about Paul Bunyan for many years. The first published stories about Paul Bunyan appeared in the early 1900s.

Famous statues of Paul Bunyan and Babe the Blue Ox are located in Bemidji, Minnesota. The statues are on the National Register of Historic Places.

Glossary

animated
made using a series of drawings, graphics, or similar artwork that looks like it is moving

legend
a famous story of the past that is not always true

lumberjack
a person who cuts down trees

monument
a structure built in honor of someone or something

orally
through word of mouth

sidekick
a friend who goes along with someone on his or her adventures

Online Resources

To learn more about Paul Bunyan and Babe the Blue Ox, visit our free resource websites below.

Visit **abdocorelibrary.com** or scan this QR code for free Common Core resources for teachers and students, including vetted activities, multimedia, and booklinks, for deeper subject comprehension.

Visit **abdobooklinks.com** or scan this QR code for free additional online weblinks for further learning. These links are routinely monitored and updated to provide the most current information available.

Learn More

Murray, Julie. *Minnesota.* Abdo, 2020.

Richmond, Marley. *Pecos Bill.* Abdo, 2024.

Van Sciver, Noah, and Marlena Myles. *Paul Bunyan.* Toon, 2023.

Index

About the Author

Heather C. Hudak has written hundreds of nonfiction children's books. When she is not writing, Heather enjoys traveling the world. She has road-tripped across much of the United States and has seen several Paul Bunyan and Babe the Blue Ox monuments along the way.